'Dazzling, angry, lucid, and shining with insight, like sunlight glinting off a fast-moving stream, this book rigorously picks apart how the digital technologies we invent to free us have impoverished our lives and invaded our minds. Julia Bell has written a book that feels like a dynamite stick. I felt cleansed reading it.' Marina Benjamin

'Terrifying, clarifying and ultimately hopeful, this is an essential book. Julia Bell grapples with the grim realities of our online lives, setting out possibilities for resisting and reclaiming our imperilled freedoms.' Olivia Laing

'This is a brilliant, beautiful and necessary essay... Julia Bell has grabbed her mind back from the "new attention industrial complex" to do the thinking and reading about what our lives online are doing to us that we all know we should be doing but seem, somehow, to be too distracted to do.' Lyndsey Stonebridge

A catalogue record for this book is available from the
British Library.

First published in 2020 by Peninsula Press

400 Kingsland Road

E8 4AA

London

peninsulapress.co.uk

Printed in Great Britain by CPI Group (UK) Ltd,
Croydon

2 4 6 8 10 9 7 5 3 1

ISBN-13: 9781999922375

Radical Attention

Julia Bell

P

PENINSULA PRESS, LONDON
POCKET ESSAYS

For all of us, in hope.

Morality is a matter of attention, not will.
We need a new vocabulary of attention.
Iris Murdoch

The formation of the faculty of attention is the true
goal and unique interest of all studies.
Simone Weil

There is no gate, no lock, no bolt that you can set upon the freedom of my mind.
Virginia Woolf, *A Room of One's Own*

San Francisco: a man pulls out a pistol on a crowded train. On the CCTV footage of that afternoon he clearly waves the gun around, points it across the aisle several times. His fellow passengers are only feet away, but no one notices him. They are all staring, scrolling, texting. The man is in the grip of some kind of mania. Clearly a danger to himself and other people. Jeopardy, chaos, terror are right there, but no one is paying attention. Not until he fires the gun into the back of the head of a disembarking passenger – killing 20-year-old student Justin Valdez – does anyone notice.

*

The early 1990s, Birmingham: I log on to my friend's Compuserve on a brand new Mac with a bright colour screen. I enter a chatroom.
Hello I type into the machine.
A beat's pause.
Hello is typed back. I remember I screamed.

*

I'm sitting in the park local to my London home. I've gone out for a walk, deliberately left my phone and wallet behind, to clear my head a little after a busy day in front of the screen. I feel dazed and dopey, my mind a blur of ideas and images. The last hour of my work time has been spent in a black hole, scrolling through webpages and social media accounts looking for – what? By the time I came up for air – a stiff neck, a pressing need to pee – I'd forgotten what I had been searching for in the first place. I was clicking uselessly into a void, pages and pages of information, none of which I was even reading, pinging between social media accounts, searches, email, my phone and laptop screens. I'd been writing, but barely got through a paragraph.

It never used to be like this when I sat down to write. I could manage three or four hours in a sitting with few lapses – maybe just a short pause, a five-minute break. Time was a continuum of attention, a satisfying thread of productivity that left me feeling as if I had achieved something real, not just dazedly lost myself somewhere, zombified by the machine. Shaking myself awake, I watch the wind stir the leaves that are curling out towards summer. I feel drugged.

It's cloudy. Cool, but not cold. The view is pedestrian: a scruffy urban park, a row of plane trees. I become aware of the people in the park around me. Everyone, apart from an old couple talking quietly to each other, and the children playing on the swings, is on their phones. Scrolling, texting. Necks bent, shoulders hunched.

My neighbours in the *meatspace* but no longer of this late spring day. A line runs through my head, in an American accent: *for your comfort and security, keep your eyes on the scenery and not on the screen.* A public safety announcement I heard repeatedly on the San Francisco Muni the last time I was there. Every journey punctuated by this phrase, followed by the hiss of brakes and the clatter of the closing doors.

I am overwhelmed by a sense of purposelessness, as if I'm waiting for something to happen but I don't know what. I'm aware that it's the tracers, the marks on my psyche that being constantly looped into a reward cycle has left behind. It's like I've forgotten how to be. Looking at my fellow citizens who can't even see me, I also feel weirdly lonely.

*

I regularly bump into people on the street who are staring at their phones. *Smombies* is the German word: Smartphone zombies. Friends have had their phones grabbed out of their hands on the street. Students, firing up their phones after class, are targeted by men on mopeds. Warning signs appear at Tube stations.

*

There is a Wikipedia page which keeps a tally of all the people who have died while taking selfies. Falling from a beauty spot, or in front of a moving train; distracted while driving, or swept off a sea wall in rough weather; or electrocuted by rail tracks, or shot by mistake. It makes for gruesome reading. Perhaps it could be cruelly funny, until you start to notice the age of those who died: 14, 17, 18, 15, 20, 16, 19, 21... A litany of tragicomic death that reads almost like Edward Gorey's *The Gashlycrumb Tinies*: 'A is for Amy who fell down the stairs, B is for Basil assaulted by bears...' It's the stuff of gothic B-movies, a warning we can't take seriously.

For your comfort and security, keep your eyes on scenery and not on the screen.

*

A few weeks after I sat in the park, Google sent me a Timeline to remind me where I had been throughout the month: Berlin, London, Tempelhof, Kings Cross, my office, my home, the houses of my friends. It told me how often I had visited these places. I was surprised by this email, unaware that I'd signed up for it through some overlooked checkbox on a page I hadn't read properly.

The one omission was the park, where I had been without my phone. I thought of that afternoon. The familiar and yet strange sight of everyone lost in their screens. The curl of wind in the leaves of the plane tree, the silence of sudden solitude. Somehow this omission was the most important part of the dataset, and the most vivid memory I had of the whole month. Unencumbered by the screen I was actually able to just be present with myself. This was the only moment when no one else had any idea at all of where I was. Where Google couldn't know where I'd been. The more I thought about it, the more comforting that realisation became.

Touch comes before sight, before speech. It is the first language, and the last, and it always tells the truth.
Margaret Atwood, *The Blind Assassin*

We are attention seekers by nature. From the moment we are born we need to connect with others. We know from the work of Winnicott and others that part of healthy cognitive development involves being given enough attention by our primary caregivers. Regulation of our need for reassurance is a part of achieving maturity. If we want to torture people, we put them in solitary confinement. Giving people the silent treatment is a classic form of bullying. In a very primal sense our bodies need to know that they are noticed by other human bodies, if for nothing else than to be reassured that we exist. As Hannah Arendt notes: 'The presence of others who see what we see and hear what we hear assures us of the reality of the world and ourselves.' We are social creatures, born into vital interrelation to other humans. The internet offers us unprecedented, new ways to connect to each other. How come, then, in the midst of this frenzy of connection, we are facing an epidemic of loneliness?

*

Italy: a man sends a woman a Facebook friend request. As a consequence, the intelligence agencies monitoring her account assume he is her husband – a notorious trafficker – connecting with his wife by pseudonym. He is quoted as saying: 'If I could go back in time, I'd cut off the finger I used to send a friend request to that woman. How could I have known she was Mered's wife? She just looked nice. That Facebook contact landed me in this absurd situation.' He has just been released after serving three years in a Sicilian jail.

*

In William Gibson's influential 1984 cyberpunk novel *Neuromancer* – which pre-existed and to a certain extent, prefigured the web – the central protagonist, a hacker called Henry Dorsett Case, is poisoned. He is given a toxin which cripples his nervous system and prevents him from accessing 'the matrix':

> Strapped to a bed in a Memphis
> hotel, his talent burning out micron
> by micron, he hallucinated for thirty
> hours. The damage was minute, subtle,
> and utterly effective. For Case, who'd
> lived for the bodiless exultation of
> cyberspace, it was the Fall. In the bars
> he'd frequented as a cowboy hotshot,
> the elite stance involved a certain
> relaxed contempt for the flesh. The body
> was meat. Case fell into the prison of
> his own flesh.

For Case, being stuck in his body is a fate worse than death, a banishment of the mind from the paradise of a fleshless cyberspace. The novel's plot hinges on him getting back into cyberspace to do one last job, thereby delivering him from the pain of his confinement within the 'meatspace' of the real world. As the internet has developed, this kind of techno-dualism has become even more clearly articulated. Technology has become a metaphor for the way in which we think about the body – the software of the mind running on the hardware of the body.

The logical end point of this is a belief in the 'singularity' – the quasi-spiritual merging of human and machine. This idea holds great sway in Silicon Valley among some of the elite: Elon Musk and Peter Thiel are believers. The theory is that one day soon, humans will merge with the machines, become bodiless, virtual creatures with a consciousness that exists somewhere in the Cloud. Perhaps it's only in a place like Silicon Valley, where bodies are so pampered and privileged and which, by all metrics, is one of the richest places on earth, that these kinds of transhumanist fantasies can emerge at all. Money and power have always led to dreams of immortality.

To me, brought up in a religious family, these fantasies of transcendence are not new, but rather a secular version of a familiar eschatology. For thousands of years religious beliefs – especially those of the Abrahamic faiths – have promoted the idea of the sinful body and the contingently forgiving God, projected somewhere in the clouds, who looks over everything and will eventually come and emancipate the believer from the prison of the flesh. Reasoning is always outsourced to God. To be human is, for the believer, to condition and orient behaviour towards this metaphysical system while at the same time ignoring and even sanctioning wilful ignorance and cruelty towards the physical body.

Writing sixty years ago, in *The Human Condition*, Hannah Arendt notes pointedly:

the future man, whom the scientists tell us they will produce in no more than a hundred years, seems to be possessed by a rebellion against human existence as it has been given, a free gift from nowhere (secularly speaking) which he wishes to exchange, as it were, for something he made himself.

Aren't these ideas of transcending our animal bodies, of a sublime union with technology, just a modern version of an ancient hubris? Of the kind that built the Pyramids, or scripted the holy texts, or told us that we would be all be living on the moon? Throughout recorded history, humans, faced with the impossible paradoxes of existence – who am I? where do I come from? why am I alive? – have sought to explain and disprove these mysteries, instead of learning to exist with the discomfort of not knowing. To be able to live with this uncertainty is one of the arts of living.

Real bodies, as the disenfranchised have always known, are problematic. Refugee bodies take up space that belongs to the entitled; queer bodies disrupt gendered norms; Black bodies challenge the structural supremacy of white bodies; disabled and sick bodies are punished for their lack of capacity to produce capital; hyper-feminised bodies are objectified and used to sell everything from cars to shampoo. Our bodies are contingent, difficult, inexplicable, messy, mortal. Instead of attending to these complexities, how much easier to pretend they don't exist at all.

*

Not so long ago a friend of mine died of a brain tumour. He lay in his hospital bed, brain dead but connected to machines that kept his organs alive. Thanks to their interventions his heart still pumped blood around his body, oxygen still filled his lungs. Above his bed were pictures of his brain scan and the black mass of his dead brain. The moment they switched off the life support, he died. The machines might have kept him alive, but they could not make him live.

*

Our attachment patterns are laid down in relation to our primary caregivers in the first few years of life. To develop into adults who have secure attachments, we need to have had our early needs met by a consistent presence – or presences – that will soothe us and feed us and pay attention to us as we unfold into the human personalities that will go on to make the adults that people this planet. The more secure the baby, the more likely it is to go on to form healthy attachments in adulthood.

The neuroscience corroborates this – as a child's brain develops, it connects pathways in the brain that lay down an internal working model of how the world will respond when there are problems. It follows by logic that a

parent who is chaotic or inconsistent or in-
different – or who vacillates between all these
positions – will likely produce a child who has
issues articulating securely their needs for attention or affection, and in dealing with rejection or conflict.

Add to this the fact that children born into
the conditions of late capitalism are born into
an environment of individual competition,
where erotic and financial capital matters
more than familial bonds. Tinder and Grindr
especially are based on an economy of looks.
Thin is better than fat, able more valuable than
disabled, tall over short, white not black, cis
not trans. Human attachment, then, as well as
being neurologically shaped by the lottery of
childhood experience, is put under pressure by
the anonymous authority of capitalism, where
the exploitation of others for personal gain
is the primary model of success. Dating apps
present us with a promise of almost unlimited
choice, while our maladaptive objectification
of others has made us weirdly fussy. In this

environment, the carousel promise of the perfect match is dangled just out of view, if you keep swiping, keep scrolling.

*

Once, in a queue in Berlin, I met an American who'd been living in Bali. He showed me his torso, a melted swirl of blue tattoos and papery-thin sliver skin. His girlfriend had left him for another man that she'd met online and taken with her their young son. Distraught and unable to process this rejection, he went on a three-day bender, poured a can of petrol over his body and set himself on fire.

*

More than one fifth of adults in the US and UK now report feeling lonely, and studies show that the stress of loneliness is as lethal as smoking 15 cigarettes a day. Our bodies don't just crave touch, we actually need it – the soothing effect of another body close to our own. It calms anxiety, and produces oxytocin, a stress-relieving peptide, released by the brain, prompted by skin to skin contact. It contributes to a feeling of general wellbeing, it protects us from stress and an early death. It is also that part of our life which is in some way unknowable: that transmission, from one human to another, which reassures us, completes us, makes us feel, however fleetingly, secure.

A friend, alone under lockdown, tells me that they find their loneliness at times overwhelming. They describe it as coming over them in convulsive, crushing waves, tangible in its intensity. In the frozen moment of lockdown, our lives were suddenly fixed in time and space. We had to face the present tense of our circumstances head on.

The pandemic peeled away the veneer of late capitalist atomisation and revealed how interlocked we actually are, how dependent on others. On small, simple actions like a handshake or a hug, or the physical presence of those who deliver our food, or work in frontline care. Life was stripped back to its mortal reality. The sudden shadow of mass death clarifying, revealing to us the nature of our vulnerable, animal bodies in all their frailty.

*

The French philosopher and activist Simone Weil thought a great deal about love and attention over the course of her short life. (She died at 34.) Her thoughts on it were laid down in some published essays, and in the letters and fragments of notebooks she entrusted to her friend Gustave Thibon before she died. Thibon stitched some of these pieces together to form *La pesanteur et la grâce* (later published in English as *Gravity and Grace*), a fragmentary sequence of meditations and aphorisms in which her thoughts on attention are interwoven with her thoughts on living a life of purpose and meaning.

For Weil, our attention has a powerful energy and agency. She argues that 'the authentic and pure values – truth, beauty and goodness – in the activity of a human being are the result of one and the same act, a certain application of the full attention to the object.' For her, attention has an importance which she equates with her own spiritual practice: 'Attention, taken to its highest degree, is the same thing as prayer. It presupposes faith and love. Absolutely unmixed attention is prayer.'

But how do we pay attention? For Weil, to really understand something – a problem, a person – we have to focus on it with the completeness of the self. Without distraction, or sentiment, or any sense of reward, and crucially without judgement. To be still, but at the same time remain open, mentally alert, active. For her, attentive looking is, in and of itself, the point: an end in itself. This is a different kind of thinking to meditation which invites you to watch thoughts come and go without asking you to consider them, or permits the ego to interpret and pre-ordain: 'attention must always be directed toward the object [...] never to the self.' This allows us to consider the object without preconceptions, our minds clear but active, open to its 'truth':

> Attention consists of suspending our
> thought, leaving it detached, empty and
> ready to be penetrated by the object.
> It means holding in our minds, within
> reach of this thought, but on a lower
> level and not in contact with it, the
> diverse knowledge we have acquired
> which we are forced to make use of.
> Our thought should be in relation to
> all particular and already formulated
> thoughts as a man on a mountain who,
> as he looks forward, sees also below
> him, without actually looking at them,
> a great many forests and plains. Above
> all our thought should be empty,
> waiting, not seeking anything, but ready
> to receive in its naked truth the object
> which is to penetrate it.

For Weil, this organic mode of thinking can elevate the most mundane realisations, allowing them to saturate the 'empty' mind: 'the most commonplace truth when it floods the *whole soul* is like a revelation.' Yet we must acknowledge that because 'our life is impossibility, absurdity,' that this process – that thinking itself – takes time, effort. We must really pay attention.

Weil's thoughts on attention were developed in relation with her teaching practice, in the alchemic space of the classroom, one of the forums in which the transformative thinking she writes about can take place. For Weil understanding can only be achieved by giving our attention wholeheartedly, especially when considering other people. Taking time to hold in our minds the whole person is the first step towards a moral, inquisitive life and the prerequisite of love. If we can learn to manage our attention, and 'renounce' our 'imaginary position at the centre', Weil suggests that:

a transformation then takes place at
the very roots of our sensibility... It is a
transformation analogous to that which
takes place in the dusk of evening on
a road, when we suddenly discern
as a tree what we had first seen as a
stooping man; or where we suddenly
recognize as a rustling of leaves what
we thought at first was whispering
voices. We see the same colours; we
hear the same sounds, but not in the
same way.

For Weil, being present, with and for other people, offers us a different way to relate to each
other. Not in competition, but in connection.
Not as atomised consumer units, but in solidarity. She advocates the kind of looking which
happens when we agree together that there are
very basic things we have in common – like
being human. When we acknowledge that our
small, weak bodies are made powerful through
their collective vulnerability rather than by try-

ing to pretend that they are in some way immune to death, sickness, fear. When we 'know', as Weil says, 'that this man who is hungry and thirsty really exists as much as I do – that is enough. The rest follows'.

*

A smartphone screen is capacitive, which means it responds to the conductive power of the human body. Which is why it can't work with fingernails or gloves. A metal coating on the glass creates an electrical field which is interrupted by touch.

When I take my broken screen into the shop to get it fixed, the man who takes my money offers three different kinds of screen. The cheapest, which is the one I pay for, has come from China. He reassures me that it's just as good as the official Apple ones which are made in Europe. He shows me the screens. They all look the same to me.

The broken screen has been cutting the tips of my fingers for weeks. While I wait for him to fix the screen under a bright craft lamp, I go for a coffee next door, worrying the jagged bits of skin on my thumbs. Usually, I would sit here and browse through my phone, now I feel naked and bored. I sip my flat white and wonder about the fact that my body is a conduit for electricity.

*

The word *screen* is both a noun and a verb: a shield, protection, an ornamental feature, a protective formation of troops, ships or planes. A site of projection, a means of obscuring or hiding something, a barrier, a boundary, a disguise. A system for sorting, for examining components. For separating wheat from chaff, for sifting soil. A barrier to insects, a preserver of modesty. A symbol of power.

*

Behind each Android screen is an accelerometer and a gyroscope, a heart rate monitor, a sensor that can detect a magnetic field.

Eric Schmidt the former chairman of Google is on record as having said that 'we can more or less guess what you're thinking about.'

*

The PornHub website now hosts over 11 petabytes of data. Played end to end, these videos translate into over 6,976 years' worth of material. Nearly seven millennia of videos of people fucking, mostly women, being fucked.

Is the effect of porn on the brain not like that of solitary confinement? Audre Lorde argues that 'pornography is a direct denial of the power of the erotic for it represents the suppression of true feeling. Pornography emphasizes sensation without feeling.'

There is something vertiginous about the abjection of that number: *seven thousand years* of porn. The trap of our objectification of others, and ourselves, where visual stimuli creates a simple physical reaction. Nothing more than a reflex; a rat, in a box, beating one out on demand for thousands and thousands of years.

*

On an Incel message board a user posts:

> I wish I wasn't ugly and short.
> That's it. I won't give some bullshit
> explanation. I just wish I looked better.
> Girls asking out chads while literally
> ignoring us. Over for us. Im 18 and
> supposed to fuck prime pussy right
> now but I don't get one fucking look
> back. I never touch these Women after
> their prime is over and they are used up.
> It's not fair, the world is just not fair.

There are other posts – many, *many* other posts – filled with self-pity and blame and fantasies of misogynistic violence. They are obscene, almost occult in their warped expressions of violence. The young men writing these rageful posts are sold on the idea that other humans – in this case, specifically women – exist only for their consumption and control.

Yet, these chatrooms and message boards are also sites of great digital self-harm, where the structures of the world are understood as rigidly oppositional. The users – many of whom show symptoms of clinical depression – get sucked into obsessive conversations about bone shape and size, trying to turn subjectively experienced aesthetics into a golden rule to make explicable their feelings of self-loathing. A perverse and masochistic community of loneliness built on the belief that whatever hurts must be true.

*

Canada: in a legal first, a teenager has been charged under terrorism offences for the fatal stabbing of a woman in a massage parlour in Toronto. Investigators determined the boy was encouraged to carry out the attack by engaging with the Incel movement online.

*

Incels have a strange relationship with love. On the face of it, they seem like disaffected Marxists. They have decided they are actors in a dating market and the distribution of resources has been unfairly stacked against them. However hard they labour, they will always be undone by their lack of capital.

The question is: how have they come to the idea that dating is a market? They are so thoroughly indoctrinated by free market capitalism they can't understand a relationship between two people that isn't transactional.

By this definition, love – and by extension via Weil, attention – is labour, and looks are capital. Once we've been sold the idea that our attention is labour, how can we learn to love in any other way?

We are drawn towards a thing because we believe it is good. We end by being chained to it because it has become necessary.
Simone Weil, *Gravity and Grace*

A friend of a friend has succumbed to an opiate addiction. For months I've been hearing stories which follow a dismally quotidian trajectory. She now has a whole litany of losses: her apartment, her business, her friends.

Her body and brain loop round in constant circles, seeking the next hit. She has become a stranger to herself and to her friends. Cocooned in her addiction, she has – temporarily – found a way to contain thoughts, stay warm, while everything else slides from view.

*

In *Hooked: How to Build Habit-Forming Products*, 'behavioural engineer' Nir Eyal describes how to initiate and manipulate behaviour in others through technology. His primer, a bestseller naked in its intentions, describes in systematic detail how to target human vulnerabilities in order to create dependence in the user.

> Emotions, particularly negative ones, are powerful internal triggers and greatly influence our daily routines. Feelings of boredom, loneliness, frustration, confusion, and indecisiveness often instigate a slight pain or irritation and prompt an almost instantaneous and often mindless action to quell the negative sensation.

Cool. Let's design an app for that.

> Habit-forming products often start as nice-to-haves (vitamins) but once the habit is formed, they become must-

haves (painkillers). Habit-forming products alleviate users' pain by relieving a pronounced itch. Designing habit-forming products is a form of manipulation.

Eyal's book opens with the claim that one third of Americans would rather give up sex than give up their smartphone. In a weird genuflection to the power of his own techniques, he then uses the example of a Bible reading app as an example of a 'good' use of his systems, the original opiate of the masses eliding with our new one.

Oh Lord, give us this day our daily push notifications.

*

I can trace an acceleration in my social media use to publication of an article. After the article was published it went viral, and for the best part of a week I was utterly overwhelmed by the demands of my phone. The constant notifications – messages, emails, tweets, trolls. It suddenly seemed urgent that I – now – respond to these at the expense of whatever else I was doing, my executive function hijacked by a primitive part of my brain. I stopped sleeping, became twitchy and reactive, a bit paranoid even. I was receiving too much attention to the point of utter overwhelm.

There is a fake urgency built into these prompts, hiding in plain sight in the language of notification settings. An 'alert' does not simply suggest new information on a topic, but a warning of danger ahead. It triggers a primal response – a state of vigilance – even if it's only to respond to a push notification from Twitter. It's a kind of biohack. Over years of use I had been trained to respond, not switch off; to be constantly on standby, ready to be called to alert. On average we check our phones every twelve minutes. Some many more times than this.

It is no accident of design that these platforms are leveraged to distract us, rather it's the logic of a system whose purpose is to capture our attention. Facebook's Like button provokes users to question their social value – is anyone paying attention to me? Being liked produces a small 'hit' of pleasure and releases dopamine, an elevation of our self-esteem, like a little bump of coke.

No wonder I am exhausted, all this information all at once – everything now – flattening intention, thought, reality. Over time, trained by the software, the user – the *user* – me – oscillates between anxiety and the alleviation of that anxiety, over and over, and bouncing between these two positions makes it impossible to think.

*

A teenager sets her family kitchen on fire while distracted by her phone. As a consequence, her mother confiscates all her devices. But the teenager figures out that she can still tweet from the console of her family's smart fridge:

do not know if this is going to tweet I am
talking to my fridge what the heck my
Mom confiscated all of my electronics again.
– dorothy ✗ (@thankunext327)

*

Nir Eyal has now written another book – *Indistractible: How to Control Your Attention and Choose Your Life* – in which he advocates methods by which we can 'hack' our own attention and reclaim what we lost to his original ideas. This paradox seems to me to be at the heart of the matter: are we to accept that we are simply manipulable brains at the mercy of our neurobiology, or are we individuals with free will? In this world of simplistic behaviourism where everything is nudged and pushed and systematised, where is the space for the personality, for thought, for that unquantifiable part of ourselves we might unfashionably call a soul?

*

In Virginia Woolf's *To the Lighthouse*, Lily Briscoe, the artist who has come to stay with the Ramsay family, whose presence disrupts and disturbs the order of things, sits alone by herself, finally, after spending a day with the family:

> For now, she need not think about anybody. She could be herself, by herself. And that was what now she often felt the need of – to think; well not even to think. To be silent; to be alone. All the being and the doing, expansive, glittering, vocal, evaporated; and one shrunk, with a sense of solemnity, to being oneself, a wedge-shaped core of darkness, something invisible to others [...] it was thus that she felt herself; and this self, having shed its attachments was free for the strangest adventures.

Where now is the space for this kind of private self? For the private reckonings, thoughts, musings, fleeting fantasies? We are so trained by the machine to respond to its prompts that time away from the screen seems empty. Increasingly, there is little opportunity for us to be with ourselves, to sink back into that invisible 'wedge-shaped' core of self. Instead, we are suddenly suspended, waiting for something to happen. It's a subtle, but terrifying, adjustment in our behaviour. When we're not online, being fed information rewards, we are still trapped by the habit of this routine. The non-digital world feels increasingly strange and perhaps even boring, because we are so used to the rhythms of click, scroll, reward.

*

After smashing my screen for a second time, I resolve to take a month off social media. After only a few days away my levels of anxiety begin to noticeably diminish. I feel more relaxed, I sleep better. I don't really miss it either, not really, though many times I find myself thought-lessly, automatically, picking up my phone. After a few weeks. I realise how I have been seeing my entire social life – myself – through the framework of a few platforms, as if I were continually playing a game. The machine is already inside my head, its structures informing and training my behaviour. I have been filtering my social choices and activity through what I think will best fit the parameters of the medium. A nice view is no longer a good photograph but a good Instagram moment. A memorable event no longer a personal memory or experience, but something to be documented for presentation on Facebook. After a month I no longer think in 280-character responses. I find myself actually reading and thinking about the news. I simply experience the world.

I feel so unburdened of my anxiety that I have started to become evangelical about it. Friends avoid me to go and lurk on social media. Among a bunch of addicts, I am the annoying one who went to rehab. But the further away I am from it, the darker it seems.

*

For the first uneasy months of the pandemic I slip back into this loop. I am checking my phone all day hungry for more information, more news. I can't focus, I struggle to read or think. I am in the grip of negative feelings, at times overwhelming anxiety, which I am looking to the information on the internet to somehow resolve. I sleepwalk through the kitchen, moving pots and pans, distractedly write a shopping list: *red peppers, tampons, spinach, fish, apocalypse.*

*The cost of a thing is the amount of what I will
call life which is required to be exchanged for it,
immediately or in the long run.*
Henry David Thoreau, *Walden*

In San Francisco in the early 2010s I met a data
miner. I was bemused by his job title. I didn't understand what that meant. To me, miners were
physical people. Men with dirty faces and black-
ened overalls exploited for their heavy labour,
who worked underground, hacking and drilling
for whatever needed extracting. This man was
hip, gamine, watchful. When I asked him what
data mining meant he said: 'I got a degree in psy-
chology and I learned how to code.'

He worked as a freelancer, designing algorithms to extract and analyse data mined from

human activity online. The efficacy of his work was judged by the amount of money he was able to make for the companies that contracted him. How well his calculations were able to analyse, predict or promote human interaction with the machine. He was stressed, he said, because there were many like him in the San Francisco of the data gold rush. Everything depended on his predictive abilities.

'But the good thing is,' he said, 'most people are really easy to manipulate. People are generally really stupid.'

A few years later, in 2017, the *Economist* announced that data was now more valuable than oil.

*

The verbs we use around attention are uniquely revealing. To pay attention describes a transaction, specifically a financial one. In French it is *faire attention* – make or do attention; in Spanish *prestar atención* – to loan attention. These differences somehow seem crucial to the way in which our different cultures think about time and value. In our mercantile, transactional Anglosphere, *paying* attention acknowledges a cost in everything we look at. Our attention is spent.

*

Pay attention! I want to shout ironically at Meenakshi Moorthy and her husband Vishnu Viswanath, teetering on the edge of a cliff in Yosemite. In the next second they will fall to their deaths while trying to take a selfie for their popular influencer account @holidaysandhappilyeverafters.

*

Our online attention is worth money because it generates data. All the things we approve of, engage with, what we search for, what we buy, what we like, who we are connected to and who they are connected to and what they share and who they share it with. The moment we interact with the interconnected machine, our behaviour is being watched and analysed.

Of course, all those complex privacy settings on Facebook are there for a reason, like the complexities of a credit agreement: to deter the user from paying too much attention – TL:DR (too long didn't read). Playful seeming quizzes and games are often blatant fronts to gather information we'd never knowingly share: our proclivities, our tendencies, our likes and dislikes, our political leanings, anything else anyone wants to know about us or our 'friends'.

Data is worth money because it can be used to generate predictions about behaviour – particularly customer behaviour. Increasingly, we have moments of algorithmic shock, where we are sure the device is listening because it has just advertised something to us that we were only just talking about – this is the predictive power of the algorithm in action.

Data scientist and ex-Facebook employee Jeffrey Hammerbacher, in a comment that he fears will be on his tombstone, says: 'The best minds of my generation are thinking about how to make people click on ads. That sucks.'

As we have used the internet more and more, the data it has on us has become more extensive and more powerful, the algorithms have now become so good at anticipating our behaviour that it's become uncanny.

All those hours of my life I'll never get back working my ass off for Facebook and Twitter.

*

An advert for a medical procedure turns up on my partner's Facebook. The advert shows an interracial lesbian couple holding a baby. It is aiming to persuade my partner to sell her unwanted eggs. It tells her how happy her 'donation' will make another couple. What seems clear from the advert is that the algorithm has identified her as a woman who is in a mixed-heritage gay relationship and has no desire to become a mother. The fee for this 'small procedure' is £700.

*

Search engines and social media corporations now have a creepy amount of knowledge, control, and power. Google now knows us better than our family, our partners or our closest friends. It knows our dirty secrets, our fears, our health scares, our middle-of-the-night terrors. What would our search history look like? What memories would it provoke? What moments of shame?

The data we have given these platforms has been used partly to sell us more stuff, and partly to train the machine – our photographs, emojis, journeys, transactions, words all used to create even more sophisticated pretentions towards Artificial Intelligence. But these datasets are leaky, insecure. They can be hacked, scraped, stolen, and sold. As data has accumulated on the servers it has given the tech companies a God-like view on human behaviour. But who gets to interpret this data? Who knows? Who decides?

*

While working with facial recognition software, MIT graduate student Joy Buolamwini noticed it couldn't identify her face because the people who wrote the algorithmic code hadn't taught it to identify a diversity of skin tones and facial structures. In an interview she says, 'I resorted to wearing a white mask to have my presence recognised.' Buolamwini calls this the 'coded gaze' and set up the Algorithmic Justice League to draw attention to bias in Artificial Intelligence software. As more decisions are outsourced to the machine, the question of who codes these algorithms matters, and without a diversity of engineers we are just baking into the system pre-existing bias and prejudice.

*

A new company called Clearview AI can match your photo to a database of more than three billion images that the company has scraped from Facebook, YouTube and millions of other websites. The company has subsequently sold this software to law enforcement agencies and private security firms.

*

In London the police announce they are going to start using real-time facial recognition software. An independent review of the police trial of the software found many problems, including its accuracy. Out of forty-two identifications made by the system, only eight were correct.

According to Big Brother Watch, the Met is the biggest police force outside China to use live facial recognition. This move also gives permission to private security companies to turn public spaces into mass biometric surveillance zones.

*

Ring, Amazon's smart doorbell subsidiary, partners with 1,300 police forces across the US. Users of the service can post videos of suspicious activity to the Neighbors app. *Motherboard* reported that posts on the app were disproportionately targeting black and brown people as criminals, and that the software was easy to hack. A family in Florida were subjected to racist abuse when a hacker gained access to their system.

*

As a consequence of the private capture of money and data, one of the fundamental distinctions which underpins a democratic society – that of the private and the public life – is reversed. We are now, if we are connected to technology, increasingly public. We are socialised to run our lives through machines, always under surveillance. We are anxious, exhausted by being so constantly on display.

By contrast, what was once public in a democratic society – the structures of government, the means by which we can affect change – is suddenly opaque, shadowy, defiant of the rule of law. Politicians are remote and corrupt, surrounded by lobbyists and unelected special advisors. Meanwhile, public funds, services and properties are privatised, controlled by a myriad of unaccountable companies, from G4S to Serco. Politics has become just another form of entertainment. Even as we express outrage and dismay about Donald Trump or Brexit or the chaotic response to the pandemic, we know these are somehow symptomatic of these new structures.

A weird kind of stasis emerges, which, as Hito Steyerl observes, 'is a very useful mechanism for a one-way redistribution of assets. What was public is privatised by violence, while formerly private hatreds become the new public spirit.' This sense of stasis is symptomatic of the overloaded, information-saturated social environment which has disrupted our ability to think, and warped our sense of time. We know that past societies had noble dreams, ambitions, ideals. They had a sense of the future. Yet life lived online is fixed by the repetitive cycles of the algorithm while years pass, even as politics becomes more chaotic, frenetic, and the climate begins to change. Meanwhile, we are still stuck in scroll, click, reward, because on screen everything looks the same.

I imagine one of the reasons people cling to their hates so stubbornly is because they sense, once hate is gone, they will be forced to deal with pain.
James Baldwin, *Notes of a Native Son*

The argument starts innocuously enough, with a flippant anti-Brexit comment on the timeline of a passing acquaintance who works for the *Daily Mail*. Before I know it, the whole thing has blown up into a frantically long and ugly argument which goes on all afternoon.

Away from the screen, I experience various conniptions from outrage, to rage, to utter contempt for this person's obnoxious views, to – finally – an exhausted kind of despair at the state of everything, at the general stupidity of people who can't see beyond their own privilege and prejudice. Unsurprisingly, it ends with

the most modern kind of social failure – an un-
friending. We can't even agree to disagree. We
fall back into our echo chambers.

*

When we are outraged our bodies are swept
up in an intense, physical feeling, raising blood
pressure, overwhelming rational thoughts.
Once triggered it can motivate us to react.
News stories seem ever more preposterous,
provocateurs even more provoking. Behind the
screen are impassive algorithms designed to
ensure that the most outrageous information
gets to our attention first. Because when we
are enraged we are engaged, and the longer
we are engaged the more money the platform
can make from us. As Craig Newmark, the
founder of Craigslist, observed in a much-
quoted interview: 'Outrage is profitable. Most
of the outrage I've seen in the online world –
I would guess 80% – someone is faking it for
profit.'

Outrageous statements will fly around the platform faster than any good news because more users engage with them. The virus of outrage gets spread by algorithms which respond, not to the actual content of the tweets, but by the amount of times people talk about it, the likes, the retweets. The creeping sourness in public discourse is caused by this, but it's happening at such a deep psychological level we can't quite work out where it's all coming from. All this unrest, this aggression. When did everyone suddenly get so pissed off?

*

Spain: a young man who dumped a fridge down a ravine is caught and forced to retrieve it. The video of him hoisting the fridge up the escarpment goes viral and attracts the opprobrium of millions of strangers. The man, who was working for some sketchy fly tippers, is now apparently in hiding, suffering from anxiety.

USA: a young right-wing extremist in El Paso goes on a shooting spree in Walmart. He leaves behind 22 dead and 24 injured and a rambling racist manifesto about immigration posted to a right-wing message board.

*

I was in a restaurant with the writer and activist Kit de Waal, when we noticed her. Sat at a table opposite us with a male companion, hyper-visible in pink athleisurewear. *Katie Hopkins.* We spoke for a long time in hushed voices about whether we should say anything. Earlier that week, in a deliberate evocation of the language of fascism, she had referred to refugees as 'cockroaches'.

What could we do – film her or call her out in some way? There seemed so many things one could say to her – physically smaller and frailer than she appears online or on TV. But it seemed obvious that if we were to do such a thing it would draw even more attention to her. It would have meant an interruption to our meal; it was annoying that we even had to notice her at all. Besides, you can't debate with a pantomime villain. All you can do is heckle. Thumbs up or down. So we tried to ignore her and left her to eat her burger in peace.

But the uncanny valley of encountering a person whose life is orientated so utterly towards hatred did not escape me. Later that night I had unsettled dreams, mixed with fantasies of shaming her into redaction and submission on social media. But these seemed as futile as my feelings of impotence in the restaurant. She, too, seemed as much a symptom as a cause of the situation we're in.

*

Content moderation is outsourced, often to companies far away from the Silicon Valley engineers who are so handsomely rewarded for their algorithms. There are many investigative reports into the conditions of people who are paid to look at the most offensive content from YouTube and Facebook. Subject to long NDAs, denied access to counselling or even unmonitored bathroom breaks, they watch deeply traumatising material for less than minimum wage, flagging and removing posts which break company rules, day after day.

At Florida-based company Cognizant, staff reportedly sat in filthy conditions for hours on end, removing graphic content posted on Facebook. In a report published by the *Verge*, one moderator reported watching a video of a man 'slaughtering puppies with a baseball bat' on just his second day in the job. The report detailed how employees were routinely subjected to videos and images of extreme child abuse, pornography, rape, torture, animal cruelty – atrocities for which they were unprepared and untrained. 'You always see death every single day,' one ex-employee commented. One moderator died of a heart attack at his desk.

*

In *Surveillance Capitalism* Shoshana Zuboff details the 'radical indifference' of the social media companies to disinformation and fake news. Anything that causes friction and stops users connecting and therefore spending more time online is not prioritized. She quotes an article by Michael Nunez in which a former Facebook product designer accuses the site of 'incentivising bullshit' by encouraging its community to self-police and report misleading content, rather than taking a more interventionist approach.

The real reason @realDonaldTrump has not been thrown off Twitter – despite clearly breaching its terms of service – is that he creates outrage, which provokes engagement. His tweets gain more impressions than any other on the platform.

By November 2019, Trump had tweeted over 11,000 times. More than half of these posts were attacks – on foreign governments, foreigners, refugees, business rivals, previous presidents, celebrities, and anyone else he perceived to have slighted him. Twitter has recently taken action by flagging some of his tweets for 'glorifying violence' and spreading voter fraud conspiracies, an inadequate penalty for an account that has over 80 million followers and reaches millions more. He uses tweets as a form of presidential briefing, circumventing the scrutiny of press conferences and interviews in favour of an unregulated platform. 'If I don't tweet it,' Trump is reported as saying, 'don't listen to my staff.'

His worth to Twitter, according to *Forbes*, is about $2bn.

*

On the left, activists have become so used to policing each other and getting outraged by lapses in 'wokeness' that they have become divided and blind to the way in which the platforms are provoking them by design. We cannot hear

another point of view because we are tricked
into convulsions of outrage which often overwhelm our ability to see that we are arguing
with our allies rather than tackling broader
injustice. Call out culture becomes a means of
being heard, but in so doing it often silences
more necessary and difficult conversations.

Consensus politics, or even any kind of politics,
becomes impossible, because we are too outraged
to actually think. So busy interacting, raging,
denouncing that we are tricked into thinking
we are actually changing something, rather than
just responding to these manufactured demands
on our attention. Add to this the amount
of disinformation being deliberately spread
through social media channels by intentionally
bad actors – foreign psych-ops, fascist-leaning
billionaires and creepy surveillance companies
– all of whom want to disrupt and confuse the
social environment.

No longer is social media the domain of happy
baby photos, or holiday snaps, or funny things
that happened while I was walking the dog, but

a full-on assault of division, disinformation, and propaganda.

*

A friend's daughter comes home from school. 'Mummy,' she asks, 'is it true that the moon landings were faked and filmed in a TV studio?'

*

The terms of democratic engagement are radically altered by this new arrangement. As well as the sheer amount of information and disinformation confusing and overwhelming the populace, the social framework – the very place in which democratic debate takes place – has moved from the real to the virtual. The connection between what we think and what is really happening becomes tenuous and unreal. We begin to have difficulty distinguishing between fact and fiction, reality and propaganda, public and private.

Our thoughts and fears are manipulated and distorted by the platforms because a system predicated on the acquisition of money above all else does not care about the truth, only what sells. So instead of reflecting a pre-existing social structure, the new structures of the internet have changed the way that people relate to each other, and to themselves. The effect on the meatspace is increasingly strange and dystopic. We know this, but it's hard to join the dots between what is happening online and what is happening IRL. And as more and more aspects of our social and professional lives are conducted online the distinction begins to lose meaning. Our lives get ever more circumscribed by the demands of capital.

Just as the dating platforms direct our attention to a very limited set of criteria (and therefore abstract the objects of our desire), the atomisation of reality brought about by newsfeed algorithms forces us to pay attention to how people *feel* about events rather than what they *think* about ideas. The debate then has no object other than to find the points at which subjectivities overlap. It's not only that we can't distinguish fact from fiction, but these are no longer the terms of the debate.

*

The UK, 2020: conspiracy theories swirl online about 5G causing coronavirus. In April alone, there are over 70 attacks on 5G masts across the UK. The Centre for Countering Digital Hate calls this an 'infovirus' which is driven by social media companies' inability to deal with false information spreading on their platforms. Over one month during the COVID-19 pandemic, volunteers flagged and reported over 649 posts containing harmful misinformation, but only 9.4% of these were met with meaningful action.

Meanwhile, researchers at King's College London and Oxford University confirm that those who believe in conspiracy theories more generally are less likely to wash their hands, accept a vaccination or a diagnostic test, or wear a facemask.

*

Our focused attention is actually quite limited. We can only really focus on one thing at a time. A bit like a computer's RAM, there is only so much capacity for processing. The present moment, neurologically, lasts for only three seconds, before the next one begins. Our deliberate attention has a limited capacity. If what we are doing is difficult then our attention is absorbed and we are unlikely to be distracted. But if what we are doing is easy then we become much more distractible.

In this environment of constant, low-level distraction our attention is often divided across many different tasks. We might scroll through Instagram while watching TV, or zone out on Facebook when we're at a bar with friends. But what is happening is that we are not actually paying attention to anything. The social media scroll or the conversation or the programme all mush into one data stream that literally passes through us, rather than being stored for future use or recall. Our capacity to make memories is most affected by this kind of divided attention. We can – just about – attend to several things at once, but we do them badly. In the midst of all the overstimulation we are unable to lay down new memories, which means we won't remember much of what we are doing either.

A new kind of human behaviour then emerges under this influence, a semi-automated for-profit personality which is being constantly nudged and notified and prompted; which is always seeking attention, always available, often anxious, often angry, afraid, jealous, paranoid, unsure of what or who to believe. The user cannot look up from the screen and notice their surroundings, because this personality, looped in a cycle of primitive fears and instincts, must always exist at pace with the algorithm. The information rewards supplant sensory attention to the actual physical body in the world. We are automating not just our actions, but also our personalities.

The technology that is supposed to free us from our flesh has actually done exactly the opposite. Rather than being liberated by technology we have become weirdly trapped in the interplay between it and our biology. We have been hacked, become hooked. Manipulations of the limbic brain for the purposes of commerce have stupefied us and taken away our capacity for thought. We are imprisoned by reactive, primitive brain activity – anxiety, self-defence, pleasure, rage, fear. Our executive functions become permanently fritzed. Smombies just scrolling through pages of information, waiting for a reaction.

*

We adopt the behaviours of an automated personality and our lives and priorities are subtly reconditioned. The cost to us all is to our individuality and our sense of time, and therefore our visions of the future; to our teenagers, a scattered, divided, anxious, sometimes violent mind; to the population, an impaired cognitive ability, information rich but attention poor; to the body politic, a kind of swirling, chaotic paranoia that makes democracy even more vulnerable to those who have figured out how to game the platforms for their own ends. Everything suddenly feels unreal, spongy. Who can we trust?

Perhaps what we're witnessing is just the beginning, the first incoherent experiments. Maybe one day there will be a generation who won't question the notion of automated human behaviour, but will accept, wholeheartedly, the idea of technology telling them what to do, where to be, monitoring and measuring every aspect of their lives. The Enlightenment idea of the human will be dead. The examined life swapped out for the monitored and programmed one. The human body transformed from a site of subjective experience, to a body in a cocoon, watched over by a machine of loving grace/controlled by authoritarian techno fascists. Perhaps both. But for a writer to whom the phenomenon, the spectacle of life is the subject, and language – as the interplay between mind and sensation – is the medium, this kind of joyless behaviourism – humans reduced to the calculus of an algorithm – seems like an unsettling, lopsided, anti-creative, unsustainable vision of the human condition.

A false friend, a friendly fraud:
both are like thieves.
Yoruba Proverb
(from *Yoruba Proverbs,* ed. Oyekan Owomoyela)

I have ordered a book from Amazon. The woman who delivers it has three children in the back of her car. They are almost submerged by parcels, their heads barely visible. She is paid per delivery. Her life is spent directed around the streets of London by an app on her phone.

*

The collision of emergent technologies with the current form of deregulated, increasingly anarchic and rapacious capitalism, has accelerated social change at a sometimes dizzying pace.

Steve Jobs said that technology should be a 'bicycle for the mind' not a means to enslave it. But then Maynard Keynes also said something similar about the economy – that it should be at the service of the people, not the means to our enslavement. The point of regulation is to regulate, like a pacemaker. A heart can only beat so fast or so slow. But, then, the heart – what is that? A part of our tiresome corporeality. Our fallible, finite, embarrassing body, and by extension our planet.

We have been seduced into thinking these technologies are inevitable, forgetting that this technology has been shaped by the attitudes of a particular set of people in a particular time and place. Predominantly white men of a certain class and education who lived (and live) in the glare of the Pacific light of Silicon Valley, influenced by the mixture of hippie idealism, Rayndian libertarianism, and gothic poverty that defines California. The ideas which structured the internet are a mixture of experiment, maths, deregulation, and money –

'move fast and break things'. Libertarian ideals provide the lure – You're an individual! Express yourself! – but the system doesn't really care if that's a photo of your cat or a suicide note. The only boundary is the one set by profit.

*

In a joke, contained in an Amazon-English dictionary hosted on Amazon's internal systems, 'Frupid' means 'so frugal it's stupid', while 'to be 'Promoted to Customer' means you got fired. During the first four months of the pandemic, Amazon made so much money that Jeff Bezos' personal fortune increased by $24 billion. Yet conditions in Amazon's fulfilment centres continue to cause controversy. Around 100 COVID-19 cases were reported at warehouses across the US, and at least eight workers were reported dead. Amazon's response to growing staff unrest was to offer a $2-an-hour temporary pay rise, which has since been withdrawn.

Julia Bell

Amazon's power to avoid tax and national oversight means that in the UK and the US it essentially operates in its own feudal system, entirely divorced from the normal rules of the nation state. Jeff Bezos is in line to be the world's first trillionaire with more power and wealth than many nations.

*

San Francisco in the early 2000s: property is cheap, the old Victorian houses made of weathered and scruffy clapboard. My sister has an apartment on the corner of Market and Sanchez, on the borderland between the Hispanic Mission and the queer streets of the Castro. The front room trembles every time a streetcar rumbles past. Even though it has rained for nearly the whole three weeks that I have been here, I have been in a state of almost constant elation: America, finally.

It is, like everyone said, familiar, like being in a movie. With its seismic hills and pretty

Victorian railroad apartments, the cable cars
and the sublime span of the Golden Gate
Bridge; Ocean Beach, at the end of the N-Judah
at sunset, the light so intense and orange that it
becomes like a black hole. Hanging out at Ker-
ouac's bar, going to the Warfield once host to
Louis Armstrong and Charlie Chaplin. Walking the same streets as Harvey Milk, soaking
up the California of Joni Mitchell and Tupac's
West Coast rap. Paying homage.

There is no iPhone yet, no Facebook, no
Twitter. But Google has just gone public and
started turning a profit. There are people on
laptops in every café working on ideas for start-
ups, something which will accelerate to almost
comic proportions in the years that are to come
– the hit sitcom *Silicon Valley* will skewer all
the fast emerging clichés of these tech bros
trying to make a buck by inventing answers for
non-problems in the hope of attracting some
venture capital. But in 2005, Silicon Valley is
regarded with both avarice and suspicion. The
first dot-com bubble burned enough people

for there to still be empty lots and broken houses across the city. The homeless are legion. Nonetheless, the city has a sense of romantic, scruffy possibility. It's also visibly gay.

There are gay bars and gyms all up this corner of Market street. The shop beneath my sister's apartment is a small leather workshop, run by two huge bears who make bespoke gimp masks and fetish wear. Gold's Gym flashes its iconic yellow neon into the night, and rainbow flags flutter everywhere – even outside the local Safeway – rainbow ribbons tied around the palm trees. This is visibility as a way of life. Since the 60s gay people from across America have come to San Francisco, drawn by its tolerance and idealism. Like Greenwich Village in New York, San Francisco is a safe space for the queers of America thrown out of their midwestern homes. My notebooks are full of hope and wonder, small town girl, glamoured by America, my new-found land.

*

An algorithm is simply a set of instructions given to a machine to accomplish a task. They are mathematical objects – equations, algebra, calculus, and so on, turned into code that the computer can understand. Human-made objects, programmed into human-made machines. Miracles of ingenuity and invention.

Ada Lovelace, the Victorian mathematician who wrote the first algorithm, and worked with Charles Babbage on the first computer, wrote: 'The Analytical Engine has no pretensions whatever to originate anything. It can do whatever we know how to order it to perform. It can follow analysis; but it has no power of anticipating any analytical relations or truths.'

One hundred years later Alan Turing addressed this assertion in his paper 'Computing Machinery and Intelligence.' In which the question becomes, not can a computer think but can a computer do what humans can do? Can a machine act indistinguishably from humans?

AI processes and technologies are now being rolled out across many systems where we expect humans to make decisions – from policing to legal services to border control. AI software is now routinely used by call centres and live chat helplines to answer simple questions about consumer experience. Many people who access customer service now would have no idea that they are speaking to a machine.

*

One of my students, Alex Graves, is an engineer for DeepMind. In a lecture on machine learning, he explains the way in which scientists are now studying how a computer pays attention to a problem. The example he uses is of handwriting recognition software, and how the machine concentrates most of its attention to the *-ing* at the end of a word in order to predict what that word might be. He shows how the machine 'reads' through a combination of contextual probability and attention. What is interesting about this lecture is the sense that the study of these processes is retroactive rather than predictive, which is ironic given he wrote the initial code. The machine has made a decision, but we no longer know how it has reached that conclusion. We have designed processes which we no longer control.

*

In the comedy show *Little Britain*, David Walliams plays a character called Carol Beer whose role is to enter questions into a computer on behalf of a consumer. Her answer, which is the punchline of every sketch, whether Carol is working in a bank or as a holiday rep or a hospital receptionist, is 'The computer says no.' Carol's sadistic unhelpfulness is shown as both a product of, and excused by, the machine. We laugh at the familiar experience of dealing with an unhelpful customer service provider who uses the computer as an excuse for being unable to help us. But there is an edge to this sketch that has persisted beyond the life of the TV show, a dystopian reality to the way in which government systems are being used against benefit claimants, or in order to police borders, or mete out credit scores: the absence of a human to whom we can petition when things go wrong.

The jobs Carol Beer pretends to do have already been superseded by the net – travel agents, bank clerks. Like the Tesco checkout workers who were paid to encourage customers to use the self-checkout, she is enlisted to usher in her own obsolescence. Once Carol has gone, the point of mediation between the customer and the machine is removed, leaving only the screen.

As artist James Bridle points out in *New Dark Age*, his compelling study of the more sinister implications of technology: 'There is also a deeper cognitive pressure at work: the belief in the singular, inviolable answer, produced, with or without human intervention, by the alleged neutrality of the machine.'

We are back in the place where we have outsourced our reasoning to a higher power: the god-like sovereignty of the machine. The computer says no.

*

A 2019 study of one of the biggest text-generating AI models discovered that it assumed that all doctors were male, and associated positive terms with Western names rather than African American ones.

*

If we allow this machine language to speak for us how much of our society, our humanity are we ceding to these new, imperfect systems? There are many ways in which – without effective regulatory, ethical intervention -- machine learning is no longer helpful, but is instead propping up what is already broken.

Hannah Arendt predicted this situation; the murderous individual is no longer the person 'just doing their job' – Eichmann's infamous excuse – but the machine:

> If it should be true that knowledge
> (in the modern sense of know-how)
> and thought have parted company for
> good, then we would indeed become
> the helpless slaves, not so much of
> our machines as of our know-how,
> thoughtless creatures at the mercy
> of every gadget which is technically
> possible, no matter how murderous it is.

Algorithms, however complex, are simply a set of instructions. They cannot replace language, our main vehicle through which we can articulate our experience of the world. Arendt again anticipates this:

> For the sciences today have been forced
> to adopt a 'language' of mathematical

symbols which, though it was originally meant only as an abbreviation for spoken statements, now contains statements that in no way can be translated back into speech.

Her point about the absence of speech is crucial, because it is only through speech that we can communicate, think, be political, act. We are more than just statistics and strings of code. However much the engineers and behavioural scientists might think they know us – and they do know a lot about us – it is impossible for them to fully describe us.

*

San Francisco, 2016: a litany of losses. It is now one of the most expensive cities in which to rent property in the USA. Tech money has taken over, the artists and the queers have been priced out of the peninsula to Oakland or even out of the Bay Area entirely. I pay my respects to the closed bars and hangouts on my walkabouts around the city. The Mission District has been slowly – then very quickly – deracinated of its Hispanic heritage. The community centred around the taquerias and burrito joints and thrift stores has been replaced by gourmet coffee, bougie clothes stores, small plate restaurants. The streets are full of a kind of young, white male, just graduated from MIT or Harvard, and Marina Girls whose expressions of femininity are handbag dogs and teetering Louboutin's. New tower blocks rise along Market (the only street without height restrictions) in a line, almost blocking out the sun. The leather shop is now a bank, the empty lot where they used to sell Christmas trees a narrow high rise; Whole Foods has encroached on Safeway, Uber is replacing the old yellow taxis that Joni Mitchell used to sing about.

Across the city there are posters everywhere: *70% of local hosts use their Airbnb money to stay in San Francisco.*

There are even more homeless, especially around Haight and in the Tenderloin. I walk the streets, like I always do when I come here, thinking, reading the weather of the place. This is not just change, but erasure.

One afternoon, tired of walking, I hail a yellow cab. On the way back to my sister's the driver rants about the state of San Francisco under the influence of Silicon Valley, the Google buses, the price of real estate, how rude and entitled they all are, straight out of their privileged college education. He tells me in a gruff drawl: 'I'd rather take my nuts and put them in a Cuisinart than work for Uber. It used to be a good thing, but now the internet's just fucking everything up.' He looks at me in the mirror, suspiciously: 'You're not one of them, are you?'

*

I go to a party, thrown by an ex-employee of one of the big social media companies.

It's in a remodelled Victorian house in a trendy part of the Mission. Money has made the host both generous and paranoid, and everyone at the party seems somehow to be in their employ – from the architect, to the sommelier, to the dog groomer, to the personal stylist, to the gardener. The host gives us a tour of the house, which includes a Versailles themed room with nothing but green flock wallpaper and a chaise longue upholstered in purple silk.

*

Lorretta Lee, a software engineer at Google who was fired in 2016, brought a lawsuit against the company for sexual harassment, discrimination, retaliation, and wrongful termination. In her deposition she says she was harassed on a daily basis. Lee's complaint detailed how she was subject to lewd comments, pranks, even physical violence:

Male colleagues spiked her drinks with
whiskey and laughed about it. Male
engineers shot nerf balls and darts at
her almost every day. On occasion, male
colleagues sent disturbing and bizarre
messages. One colleague sent her a
text message asking if she would like
a 'horizontal hug.' Another showed up
at her apartment with a bottle of liquor
and offered to work with her to fix a
problem she was having with one of her
devices.

During a party she was slapped in the face by a
drunk colleague for no apparent reason. One of
them crawled under her desk so he could look
up her skirt. Lee had begun working at Google
when she was 26: 'this bro-culture was the
only professional environment she knew'.

Since this case was brought, many others
have come forward. On her blog in a post title
'Life as a Female Techie', Lee writes: 'In a word:
LONELY.' A reality compounded by the fact that

around 18% of engineers are women – a percentage that has gone down since the 80s, not up.

*

A memo from Google engineer James Damore is leaked. In it he complains about Google's diversity drives, which he perceives as pointless because, in his view, men are just better at engineering:

> Women, on average, have more:
> Openness directed towards feelings and aesthetics rather than ideas. Women generally also have a stronger interest in people rather than things, relative to men (also interpreted as empathizing vs. systemizing).

*

Tech journalist, Emily Chang, in an interview about her book *Brotopia: Breaking Up the Boys' Club of Silicon Valley* comments: 'I vividly remember this one male investor who said to me that's not a book, that's biology.'

*

A survey carried out by the Commons Women and Equalities Committee has revealed that two thirds of a hundred and seventy UK politicians who responded are being abused and receiving death threats online. Mostly women, mostly on Twitter.

*

Writing in an essay for the Cato Institute, Peter Thiel, CEO of surveillance company, Palantir, revealed that he no longer believed that freedom and democracy were compatible:

> The vast increase in welfare
> beneficiaries and the extension
> of the franchise to women – two
> constituencies that are notoriously

tough for libertarians – have rendered the notion of 'capitalist democracy' into an oxymoron.

*

There has been a major data breach in a biometric facility belonging to a company called Suprema. On their website, Suprema describes itself as 'a global Powerhouse in biometrics, security and identity solutions.' Their products include 'biometric access control systems, time and attendance solutions, fingerprint live scanners, mobile authentication solutions and embedded fingerprint modules.'

In increments, our world begins to take on the names and events of dystopian fiction, there is the growing suspicion that the reality that is being imagined for us is not one which we own. If the world is being programmed by only one kind of mind. What happens to the rest of us?

*

Iran: the internet is effectively entirely blocked during an uprising. Amnesty International estimates over 200 have died at the hands of the regime but this figure is impossible to verify. Meanwhile the regime rolls out a country-wide Intranet which can deal with banking and other networked functions of the state.

*

There is a huge power cut across the UK which leaves passengers stranded in stations and on trains. My power goes off for half a day, the freezer starts to defrost. I wonder if I have enough candles for the evening, whether I should be stockpiling. I am moved to look up survival kits on the internet before I realise my wifi is also down. I can still connect to the internet by my phone but the battery is running out. I end up flicking through an old SAS survival book I bought from a charity shop years ago, read up on the section about dipping matches in wax to make them waterproof.

According to the Paris-based think tank The Shift Project, 4% of all carbon emissions can now be attributed to global data transfer and the infrastructure necessary to support it. Video makes up over 80% of the traffic. I wonder how much of this is porn.

*

In London the number of gay bars and clubs has dropped dramatically from 121 to 51. The internet has created spaces online for people to meet, rendering the old sites of visibility redundant.

But in China, a crackdown on LGBTQ topics on the microblog Weibo led to the closure of the 'les' discussion group for lesbians.

In Tanzania, names of LGBTQ people have been spread through WhatsApp. Many have been forced into hiding.

In Egypt, authorities use dating apps to entrap gay men and lure them to hotel rooms where they are then arrested in an ongoing crackdown against homosexuality.

Across the UK reports of anti-gay and lesbian hate crimes have more than doubled in five years. Stonewall links this to an emboldened right-wing which is loudly circulating its propaganda online.

*

Alice Bergmann's sister was killed by an immigrant. Alice is from Chemnitz. She supports Bayern Munich, likes animals and is a fan of Leonardo DiCaprio. She also posts many sad updates about the death of her sister and how much she hates immigrants. But Alice's profile photo is of Chilean actress Josefina Montané.

The profile is a fake 'sock puppet' account, set up and maintained by a network of extremists looking to stir up anti-immigrant sentiment.

While Facebook boasts that it has 2.45 billon active monthly users, the company discovered and deleted around 5.4 billion fake profiles in 2019 alone.

Advances in machine learning mean that computers have developed an even more sophisticated ability to write text like humans. A language model trained on right-wing manifestos can formulate convincing tweets and chat comments. Deepfake videos become even more plausible and difficult to spot. Machine generated content can overwhelm websites and forums with fake likes and news. On a website called This Person Does Not Exist you can create unique, realistic-looking photos of people who will never exist.

*

I talk on the phone with a friend who has two teenage daughters. I ask her how she deals with their access to the internet. She sighs and tells me they spend hours watching videos on

YouTube of people unwrapping Kinder eggs. 'I tell them, it's not your friend.'

To be in touch with senses and emotions beyond
conquest is to enter the realm of the mysterious.
bell hooks, *Outlaw Culture*

Our attention lies on a new frontier between the public and the private. Whereas before it might have been property that gave us privacy – a home, physical sanctuary – now it must almost be at the level of our consciousness that we decide whether we are in public or private. As the pandemic has forced many to work from home, it has exposed the extent to which these spaces are increasingly virtual designations. In an environment where we Zoom from our sofa we have less and less connection to our place within the physical world. When do we check our phones in the morning – before or after we pee? But what of our bodies? What about our racing heartrates, our sweaty palms, our corporeal selves?

*

There has been an explosion of mindfulness meditation, as a means of self-soothing, calming the brain, and reducing symptoms of anxiety. This has been driven, unsurprisingly, by Silicon Valley. Essentially Buddhist meditation decoupled from religious practice, it requires counting the breaths, allowing the body to calm, letting the rhythms of the mind settle. It has a proven, if limited, palliative effect on the brain yet there are a thousand apps for it now. One of the biggest selling apps is Headspace, which has 40 million downloads worldwide and over 1 million paid subscribers. It is valued at over $1 billion.

But while it can help to momentarily calm the anxious mind – it is essentially a passive solution. In soothing tones, these apps clear away some of the mental clutter but don't invite you to consider *why* you might be so anxious or overwhelmed.

What conditions create this reality? What about this overwhelming, overheating world might need changing? After all, reality is just thoughts and thoughts just come and go...

We are sold the idea that our anxieties are simply a consequence of too many thoughts, even while our thoughts and actions are being nudged and pushed and engineered from underneath us by technology. Which creates a strange dissonance: when we're told to override our anxious feelings and to both think more and *less*, what is normal functioning?

Distraction and mindfulness then become two sides of the same coin. In Silicon Valley's behaviourist terms we can overcome inbuilt distractions by scheduling ourselves and using apps to help us focus. But this is only to allow us to continue to reproduce the personas that create profit for their companies. The emphasis on individual self-control at once elides and acknowledges that everything we do is simply a consequence of biological triggers, reducing a human being to a set of mechanisms which can be hacked, tweaked and triggered. It decouples the useful, contemplative, humanist aspects of meditation from its spiritual practice and re-packages it as a solution to a problem that we created in the first place. Meditation becomes just another means of self-optimisation, of pol-ishing ourselves ready for a life inside a Sili-con Valley Instagram feed, a place which bears very little resemblance to our actual lives. This approach doesn't work to solve the ethical and intellectual questions posed by the unsettling reality of what technology, as it is currently uti-lised, is doing to the organisation of society and to ourselves. To the reasons why we might be anxious. For that we need a different kind of at-tention, a more radical, *active* kind of attention.

*

When we engage in creative thinking – defined as being able to make deep and wide-rang-ing connections between disparate ideas and objects to form new ideas – it requires a new kind of attention. Attention which involves being able to critically analyse a situation for its hidden structures and present a layered and nuanced portrait of a character or a world. It involves working with words and meaning, having a rapacious curiosity: asking questions. It goes back to Keats' notion of 'negative capability', being able to exist within conundrums, paradoxes, and to resist the temptation towards absolutes, to understand nuance. Writing in this way is an active, productive kind of attending. It demands full concentration, a willingness to push and question orthodoxies and received opinions, to consider the alchemic power of language.

In the digital, we are to an extent all writers now. There are an estimated 3 trillion words written online every day. It creates a kind of public thinking where people are less inhibited or guarded than they might be in the social sphere because they are screened from reality. Hyperbole abounds in clickbait headlines, as does the language of piety and bragging, and oversharing and outright lying. And it has created a new language of symbols, emojis, gifs, and shorthand. We are drowning in language but unable to articulate a common reality. It's all very well having all this capacity to connect but what do we want to achieve with it?

As Gilles Deleuze observes in *Negotiations*:

> we're riddled with pointless talk,
> insane quantities of words and images.
> Stupidity's never blind or mute. So
> it's not a problem of getting people to
> express themselves but of providing
> little gaps of solitude and silence in
> which they might eventually find
> something to say. Repressive forces
> don't stop people expressing themselves
> but rather force them to express
> themselves; what a relief to have
> nothing to say, the right to say nothing,
> because only then is there a chance of
> framing the rare, and ever rarer, thing
> that might be worth saying.

Julia Bell

What we lose in all this talk is the generative, creative space of not knowing, the place of possibility that Keats so well understood. When we are called, day after day, to have an opinion, we are denied the time and space and crucially the silence we need to think.

*

We have forgotten, or maybe, thanks to the effects of climate crisis and the coronavirus pandemic, we are remembering, that we are primarily bodies in an organic world. One which is being trashed by unregulated capitalism which centralises and distributes everything in a way which might be efficient for the machine, but which is disastrous for human – bodily – freedom. Technology tells us we're connected to people all over the globe, even while global borders are tightened around us, and narratives which otherize and polarise those whom we perceive as not of our communities loudly proliferate. Increasingly, we have no reason to leave our homes. We can work remotely on our laptops, have food and products delivered, and the external world, degraded and full of the disenfranchised and infectious, becomes frightening. We are losing our trust in each other, in our ability to find common ground.

We need to return to the simple fact that experience comes to us from our senses. From what we smell and touch and see and hear and feel through our bodies. Through what happens to our bodies. Through the bodies that live around us. Attention to the way in which the body processes sensory experience is the most effective, and most obvious, way to look beyond the screen that technology has put between us and our understanding of the world.

*

Simone Weil, who taught philosophy of science at the Lycée for Girls in Le Puy, understood that teaching involved the training of attention.

Attention, more than any other skill was for her 'the object of all studies'. This kind of attention involves not just distancing ourselves from the thing observed, but from our own powers of observation.

> Above all, our thought should be empty, waiting, not seeking anything, but ready to receive in its naked truth the object which is to penetrate it. All wrong translations, all absurdities in geometry problems, all clumsiness of style and all faulty connection of ideas [...] all such things are due to the fact that thought has been seized upon some idea too hastily and thus being prematurely blocked is not open to the truth.

This kind of teaching is at odds with the sort of skills-based training being encouraged by our current education systems, which are being ideologically driven by those who would have us think less and work more.

Weil believed – and proved through her own work – that freedom was about the relationship between thought and action, and that attention was the vehicle for that transmission. People were most oppressed when they had no time to think, which was the condition of most of the workers she encountered in the impoverished parts of France that she lived and worked in. And education, which focused on training, not knowledge, even further encouraged this kind of oppression.

Weil says in a letter to a colleague that her students had 'no idea either of the connection between the sciences or of the methods by which they were created.' In other words, that sciences are not objective thought processes but come to us through history and experiment, 'something human, instead of a dogma which you have to believe without ever really knowing why.'

Within the institution, market forces are now reiterating the importance of 'employability' and value in education as if the only metric of a good education is whether you can get a job, not whether you will be an engaged, questioning human being. This means that humanities subjects are suffering a sharp decline – history, literature, languages, philosophy swapped out for STEM subjects.

This is happening in congruence with conversations around the gamification of learning, a move to online learning only accelerated by the pandemic. This involves turning hour-long seminars into shorter activities – quizzes and interactive tasks, some of which can be done on the phone.

These strategies are of limited use in a humanities seminar. In many ways they are antithetical to the kind of attention that the teaching of literature or philosophy or writing is trying to engender, where the point is to read and think deeply about a problem with the other students in the room. Thinking together in this way is transformative. It invites, slow, careful, thoughtful questions. Awkward moments of revelation too. But in an atmosphere where no question is invalid, we start to see past knee-jerk reactions and actually listen to our common concerns.

In my teaching practice I see that the acquisition of this kind of attention is often revelatory to the students who come to study with me. I work to draw the attention of my students through a set of problems, almost exactly as one might draw a line on a page, trying to instil in them attentive practice, a capacity for concentration, so that they can make connections, *think*, and engage in the kind of deep reflection that good writing, but also good living, demands.

Enabling this kind of thinking – what Weil calls 'gymnastics of the attention'– is where access to knowledge and discovery lies. Training the attention in this way also enables moral perception, which means we can choose how we respond to the world. We can know more, even if we focus on less information. We can ask more searching questions, draw connections between ideas, we can even, perhaps, begin to find solutions. As Weil suggests: 'We do not have to understand new things, but by dint of patience, effort and method to come to understand with our whole self the truths which are evident'.

But it is the exercise of this reflective, embodied thinking which has become increasingly obscured by the screen. When you start to put the effects of technology under the glare of considered attention – the whole thing starts to become uncanny, surreal. Disturbing, even. It becomes clear that our attention – our capacity to decide what we observe – is one of the critical frontlines in our new, dystopian reality. Connected technology, the internet, as currently mediated by corporate monopolies, is, to use Timothy Morton's word, a 'hyperobject', something which is happening to us – around us – but which is abstract, covert, and almost too immense to comprehend.

To counter this, we need a radical attention that understands consciousness is still harnessed to flesh. Bodies that are mutable, strange, contingent, and mysterious. Attention means that we must in return honour that mystery in each other. In a world in which everything is explicable, where is the space for wonder?

Iris Murdoch, picking up on Weil's ideas forty years later, writes in *The Sovereignty of Good* that 'unsentimental, detached, unselfish, objective attention' is a prerequisite to the ability to perceive what is true. Murdoch secularises Weil, turns God into Good, but the basic idea of attention remains the same – that it is a capacity for looking at the world in a way which overrides the ego, and which allows us to change the quality and effect of our consciousness. As Murdoch writes: 'Freedom, we find out, is not an inconsequential chucking of one's weight about, it is the disciplined overcoming of the self.'

In a political climate where lies and distortion and anti-social tendencies are pre-requisites to power, this kind of attentive looking takes a certain kind of moral courage. It's a capacity which we must all learn to exercise like a muscle. Changing the messy present – devolving power, decentralising, living more simply, being at peace with the planet – won't come without action, or effort. Without thought. To change the status quo we need to make our bodily presence felt, and exercise our freedom to act, and to think, especially now, while we still have the power to do so.

Sometimes the best way to glimpse meaning is to start small, to pay attention to detail, and give your deliberate attention to what is in front of you. To try and notice what happens. To make time. To choose to look.

*

The late composer and activist Pauline Oliveros engaged in a practice that she called 'deep listening'. Basically, listening to sound with the whole body. Like Weil's notion of attention as a bodily act, Oliveros posits the same idea in her *Meditations*, suggesting that her listener-participants 'walk so silently the bottom of your feet become ears.'

For Oliveros, listening was a political act, a means of resistance, of attending to the body, being alive to its sounds as a way to generate change and to heal. She came up with her sound experiments at a time of deep political despair, when the Vietnam war atrocities and protests were at their height. She describes feeling a tremendous fear, of going inwards to defend herself from its assaults. To her, listening was a pause before action: 'Listening is directing attention to what is heard, gathering meaning, interpreting and deciding on action.'

I try to engage writing students in a similar kind of practice, to sit and look at something – a photograph, an object – until the act of looking becomes boring, almost unbearable, because it's only under these conditions that the nature of the object begins to reveal itself. What is overlooked in the hurry to get to the next thing is suddenly obvious. Moments of grace, insight, and wisdom become possible. Language begins to flourish, creative associations, solutions, and speculations blossom. As Weil puts it: 'by pulling at all the bunch, we make all the grapes fall to the ground.'

It is this kind of productive, creative attention we need now. Being totally present with ourselves, and with each other, is an active form of hope. It's a line of defence against the propaganda machines that threaten to pitch us into new and alarming conflicts; against the personality-warping effects of social media; against the insatiable demands of a capitalism that requires us to constantly perform versions of ourselves; against the dark hearts of the forces that are ranged against us. Attention to the body, and by extension to the planet, to the miracle of its aliveness, allows us to reconnect to the parts of ourselves that have been out-sourced to the screen

Like Arendt, I am asking only that we make space to 'think what we are doing' both for ourselves and for each other, because if we don't, those with very different visions of society will prevail in the coming struggle.

Julia Bell

*

In a moving essay about Chekov's short story 'The Kiss', James Wood makes the case for what he calls the 'serious noticing' of literature. The way in which both writer and reader are drawn to the telling details, the small transcendent moments that exist in literature and in life, when we are alive to our senses, to what happens around us. Whether we like it or not, those of us who wish to argue for the humane in humanity are engaged in a battle with forces which would seek to subdue us – for profit, for power, for sadism. We are increasingly going to have to stand up to defend ourselves. We are going to need to engage in even more radical forms of attention, to get off the net and into the streets and the classrooms, to offer up new, practical solutions to the common problems we all face. We are going to need to find new ways to come together, rather than succumbing to the fake pressures of our online identities.

Black Lives Matter erupted out of a pandemic that felt – to those of us not on the front line – weirdly virtual. The protests are a loud reminder that bodies matter. That our bodies still have great collective power, on the streets, in protest, in solidarity, as well as in silence, withdrawn, deliberately withheld. The pandemic has exposed the cracks in the machinery and as such has led to an outpouring of rage against the system. This is perhaps one of the few means we have left of changing things, as a wholehearted, conscious body in the world: on strike, in protest, in defence, in defiance, in solidarity, in the way. Fully attentive, radically alive, aware of our physical vulnerability. Whatever the future holds, while we have breath we still have choices about what we attend to, and attending to the miracle of our consciousness in the world – allowing ourselves to experience our individual, wedge-shaped core of darkness, without being nudged or pushed or spied upon – is the most difficult, necessary, and radical act of all.

Acknowledgements

I am aware of the irony of the fact that this book would not have been written without the internet, without the free access to knowledge and information provided by its platforms. And I am also aware of the kind of discipline it took to stay on track with my topic of research there were so many rabbit holes which opened up, as the more I looked the more there seemed to be to see. If this book achieves anything it is to encourage the reader to do some attentive looking of their own. All facts are taken from places of public record and where possible have been double checked. I also read a great deal of books; the most important ones are listed in the bibliography.

This would not have been written without the support and encouragement of many people, but chiefly among them, my beloved Golnoosh Nour who encouraged me from the beginning with this project. Big thanks are also due to Jean McNeil and Emma Hargrave who read drafts of this work in progress. Richard Hamblyn for his ever-supportive collegiality. Professor Chris Frith clarified some of my questions about the neuroscience, and Alex Graves and Dr David Plans gave me helpful comments and suggestions. Thanks to Jake Franklin, Sam Fisher, and Will Rees at Peninsula for giving me this opportunity and being attentive and ambitious readers, and for daring to run a small, radical press in these dark times. We owe them our thanks, support, and solidarity.

Selected Bibliography

Arendt, Hannah – *The Human Condition*
Bridle, James – *New Dark Age*
Chang, Emily – *Brotopia*
Deluze, Gilles – *Negotiations*
Eyal, Nir – *Hooked*
Fry, Hannah – *Hello World: How to be Human in the Age of the Machine*
Gibson, William – *Neuromancer*
hooks, bell – *Teaching to Transgress*
Lorde, Audre – *Your Silence Will Not Protect You*
Morton, Timothy – *Hyperobjects*
McNamee, Roger – *Zucked*
Murdoch, Iris – *The Sovereignty of Good*
Purser, Ronald – *McMindfulness*
Steyerl, Hito – *Duty Free Art: Art in the Age of Planetary Civil War*

Tolentino, Jia – *Trick Mirror*
Weil, Simone – *An Anthology; Gravity and Grace*
Williams, James – *Stand Out of Our Light*
Zuboff, Shoshana – *Surveillance Capitalism*

Peninsula Press would like to thank Larry Coppersmith and Dominic Franklin for their continued support.